Riddles, Riddles Everywhere

by Ennis Rees

illustrated by Quentin Blake

ABELARD-SCHUMAN
New York

Printed in the United States of America

On land and sea and in the air,
  Riddles, riddles everywhere.
Right here in this book you'll find a few—
  For example,
    What's little
    And likes a clue?

A riddle
And you.

Tell me now
What is it that
Is over your head
And under your hat?
Your hair.

The answer to this
   Is slightly absurd,
But why is a horse
   Right much like a bird?

   Haven't you ever seen a horse-fly?

*

Some days are rainy,
   Some days are fair.
Friday comes before Thursday—
   Where?

   In the dictionary.

*

Explosions all over the nation
   Bring this question to mind.
Where was the Declaration
   Of Independence signed?

   At the bottom.

*

If a tree broke a couple of windows
   Way up high,
Do you know what the windows
   Would probably cry?

   "Tree, mend us!"

Holes fastened to holes,
Chilly to feel,
Mostly empty,
But strong as steel.
A chain.

Though it's close to your eyes,
  You'll have to admit
It's hard to get more
  Than a glimpse of it.

Your nose.

*

I tremble and shake
  At the least breath of breeze,
Yet I can take
  As much weight as you please.

Water.

*

A lady stays
  On yonder hill
Who rocks and sways
  And never stands still.

A tree.

*

A man rode to town on Thursday
  And stayed all night at the inn,
Then rode home upon the same Thursday.
  How could such a marvel have been?

He rode a horse named Thursday.

Bim, bam, blamity, blee,
Children make something that no one can see.
Noise.

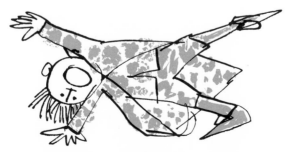

When the bank goes broke
　That isn't funny,
But what kind of bank
　Needs no money?
　　　　A river bank.

*

　　What time is it
　　　When the hallway clock
　　Strikes thirteen
　　　And starts to knock?
　　　　　Time to have the clock repaired.

*

Tell me the answer
　To this if you will.
When will water
　Stop running downhill?
　　　When it gets to the bottom.

*

　　　If Miss Issippi,
　　　Known as Skippy,
　　　Gave Miss Ouri,
　　　Full of fury,
　　　Her New Jersey
　　　To wear at the fair,
　　　What, oh what
　　　Would Dela Ware?
　　　　　I don't know, but Al-ask-a.

14

Walk on the living,
    They don't even mumble.
Walk on the dead,
    They grumble and grumble.
        Green leaves and dry leaves.

If two's company and three's a crowd
And bees live in a hive,
Tell me, now, for crying out loud,
What are four and five?

Nine.

*

What would happen very soon
If you swallowed your cereal spoon?

You wouldn't be able to stir.

It may be that you'll doubt your luck
When the answer to this is found,
But tell me why a baby duck
Walks softly on the ground.

Because it can't walk, hardly.

What has four fingers and a thumb
  But neither flesh nor bone,
Is small or large or medium
  But seldom is alone?

A glove.

Full all day,
    Empty at rest,
Both of us
    Are very hard pressed.

A pair of shoes.

*

What country do you become,
    Or so I've been told,
On a morning when fingers are numb
    Because it's so cold?

Chile.

*

What never asks
    Any questions at all
Yet often is answered
    By short and tall?

The telephone.

*

Tickle Tockle continues to run
    And wave his hands in the air,
But though he runs in shade and sun
    He never gets anywhere.

A clock.

Little white birds
   Float down through the air
And light in the trees
   When they are bare.

Snow.

19

What island was largest
   On earth anywhere
Before Australia
   Was known to be there?

Australia.

*

When crossing a desert
   Why is it that,
Though you don't get hungry,
   You might get fat?

Because of the sand which is (sandwiches) there.

*

Though this one's a wow,
   It might make you ill.
Why does a cow
   Go over a hill?

Because she can't go under it.

*

Though they have been known to be trippers
   And some by them have been hurled,
What make the very best slippers
   Of all the things in the world?

Banana peels.

A shiny, long, blue-black fellow,
Pull his tail and hear him bellow.

A gun.

21

A man lost his dog in the woods
   And searched in vain.
How at last out there in the woods
   Did he find him again?
      By listening to the bark all around him.

If you crawled into a hole
And dug, dug, dug like a mole
And like a mole wiggled your snout,
Where finally would you come out?

Out of the hole.

*

Click your heels
And cut a caper,
Then say what the pen
Said to the paper.

"I dot my eyes on you."

*

This one has often been guessed
By short and tall.
How did the woodman request
His tree to fall?

He just "axed" it.

What can go through
  The water and yet
Not ever become
  The least bit wet?
        Sunlight.

* *

Why did the farmer
  All in fun
Name his rooster
  Robinson?
        Because he Crusoe.

* *

Have you the slightest notion
What bus crossed the ocean?
        Columbus.

* *

What did the near-sighted porcupine say
When he backed into a cactus one day?
        "Excuse me, honey."

* *

What animal,
  Somewhat a glutton,
Is able to
  Go round a button?
        A goat is able to go round a-buttin'.

When you buy eggs on a farm
When out for a ride,
How can you be sure that they have
No chickens inside?

Buy duck eggs.

25

Guess this for me
As best you can.
How long should be
The legs of a man?

Long enough to reach the ground.

*

I'll give you a hug
And then one more
If you guess what the rug
Said to the floor.

"Hands up! I've got you covered."

*

Answer me this, I pray,
And do be bold.
What do crows do when they
Are three years old?

Start their fourth year.

*

When the old hen laid
An orange one day,
What did the little
Chicken say?

"Oh, see the orange mar-ma-lade!"

I give to you
　　My best regards.
Now why are wolves
　　Like playing cards?

They both come in a pack.

Next time at the shore
    I'll play you some ball
If you guess what the floor
    Said to the wall.

"I'll meet you at the corner."

*

Here's a thorny sort of riddle.
What did the big rose say to the little?
"Hiya, bud."

What lies out back   I know a little fence
    As quiet as can be,   That's white and wet,
But begins to hack   * But it's never been painted
    When it gets to a tree?   Nor rained on yet.

An ax.   The teeth.

I tell people their faults,
    Though I can't make a sound.
Even so, they must like me, for always
    They keep me around.

A mirror.

Mickle, trickle, eat a pickle,
   What is there besides a nickel
That will very surely tickle
   Everybody, firm or fickle?
A feather.

Which animal travels lightest
   And which one carries the most,
Whether the trip be just a mile
   Or a journey from coast to coast?

The rooster takes only his comb, but the
elephant always brings his trunk.

Who are the two from whom we beg
  As long as we're living
And who, though neither has arm nor leg,
  Keep giving and giving?

The earth and the sea.

*

A great green house,
  Wealthy and wide,
The wind blows across it—
  Deep quiet inside.

The sea.

*

If now you miss this riddle,
  Perhaps you'll guess it later.
What is it that stays hot longest
  In the refrigerator?

Pepper.

*

I have a garden
  Of blossoms bright
That never bloom
  Except at night.

The sky and the stars.

31

Begins with a P,
　　Ends with an E,
Has a thousand or so
　　Letters, I know.

The Post Office.

*

When babies are at rest
What land do they like best?

Lapland.

*

What should you do
　　When out of hope
You finally come
　　To the end of your rope?

Tie a knot and hang on.

*

Answer this
　　And you're going some.
From what country
　　Do fish come?

Finland.

*

What did the mother ask
　　Her crying child,
And what did the child reply
　　That's just as wild?

Mother: "Are you Hungary?"
Child:　"Yes, Siam. May I have a slice of Turkey?"
Mother: "Hawaii now?"
Child:　"I'd like Samoa."

Full of beats,
   Wears a cowhide cap,
And never speaks
   Till you give it a slap.

A drum.

Big enough
    To hold a pig,
Small enough
    To be held like a twig.

A pen.

*

                    There were 710
                    Women and men
                    At sea in a boat
                    That ceased to float.
                    When it spun around
                    And turned upside down,
                    What was left then
                    Of the 710?

OIL.

*

Which weighs more,
    When all has been said,
A pound of feathers
    Or a pound of lead?

They weigh the same.

*

            I have a pink pen
                That I keep full
            Of glossy white cattle
                And one red bull.

My mouth, my teeth, and my tongue.

34

The ground was white,
The seed was black.
Guess it you might.
You're on the right track.
Paper and ink.

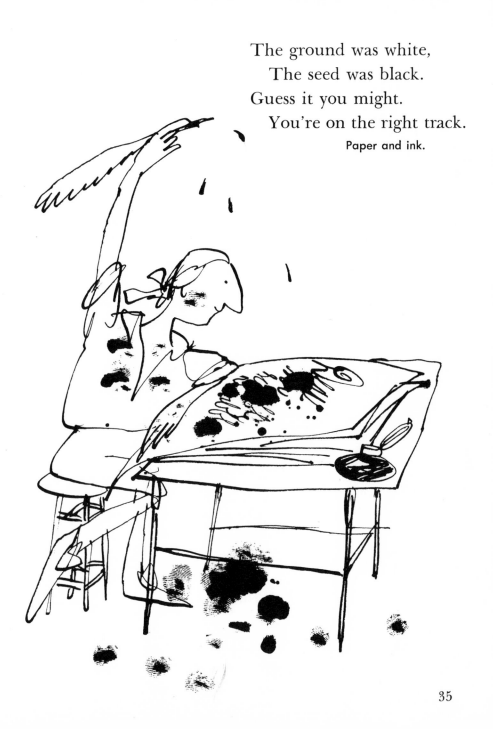

Chinka-chinka-chinka-pen,
What's trampled on by millions of men?
Shoes.

*

Round as a wheel,
  Hollow as a cup,
Forty thousand elephants
  Couldn't pull it up.
A well.

*

Why were the Egyptians,
  Beside the Nile waters,
Such excellent sons
  And dutiful daughters?
Because they had great respect for their mummies.

*

What can you hold
No matter how old
In your left hand
That you can't hold
No matter how bold
In your right hand?
Your right elbow.

*

Above the ground,
  Not in a tree.
I've told you the answer—
  Now you tell me.
Knot in a tree.

Answer this riddle at once
And please don't wait.
What is the hardest thing
About learning to skate?

The ice.

Three birds sat on a fence
Taking the air.
Now what is the difference
Between here and there?
The letter T.

*

It very well may be
That you are a beginner,
But tell me what's the best way
To get a duck for dinner.
Go jump in the lake.

*

Which is better
In country or town—
"The house burned up"
Or "The house burned down"?
Either is pretty bad.

*

Has eighty-eight keys
And needs no more
But can't unlock
A single door.
A piano.

I really don't mean
  To give you a scare,
But when is a boy
  Most like a bear?

When he is barefooted.

Though not a soldier,
   I often fight.
Though not a musician,
   I sing before light.
Though not a clock,
   I wake people up.
What am I, then,
   If I'm not a pup?

   A rooster.

*

What kind of coat
   Has never yet
Been put on well
   Any way but wet?

   A coat of paint.

*

Here's one that you can ask an ape.
Which is the bluest side of a grape?

   The outside.

*

Can't walk
   But runs very well,
Can't talk
   But makes people yell.

   A taxi cab.

Why do you suppose
   It would be all wrong
If your pretty nose
   Were twelve inches long?

Then it would be a foot!

41

I walked until
    At last I got it,
But liking it not
    I stopped to spot it,
And when I found it,
    I said "That does it"
And threw it away.
    So now what was it?

A splinter in my foot.

*

Four legs and a back
    But body none.
When you sit on a tack
    You're close to this one.

A chair.

*

When building my house
    I never shirk,
But with my mouth
    I do most of the work.

A bird building her nest.

If you had to give your things away
  And didn't know what to start with,
What single item would you say
  Is the easiest thing to part with?

A comb.

*

Riddle me this and try not to grin
  Because it's so easy to see.
What did most American men
  And women used to be?

American boys and girls.

*

Missy, Missy,
  Golly, gee,
What has four eyes
  But still can't see?

The Mississippi.

Brownie, Brownie, much admired,
Many a horse have I tired—
Many a horse and many a man,
Riddle me this one if you can.
A saddle.

*

Have you heard the yarn
That's going around
About the two darn
Big holes in the ground?
Well, well.

*

Spring, I suppose,
Is the very best time
For people who picnic
To eat in the woods,
But tell me who knows
The very best time
For people to pick
To read in the woods.
When autumn turns the leaves.

*

What can't walk a step, but matter of factly
Possesses a hundred legs exactly?
Fifty pairs of pants.

Why do girls
Like to wear
Pretty ribbons
In their hair?

Because they like bows (beaux).

If you bounce a green pea
  Off a bass drum
And into the sea,
  What will it become?
    Wet.

*

What animal drops from the clouds
And splashes all over crowds?
    The rain, dear.

*

Two boys went hunting and shot a jay
  Which they brought home and cooked all day.
Then they ate the bird with a sliced cucumber.
  What was the two boys' telephone number?
    281J.

*

I have a little sister,
  They call her Twinkle Toes.
She dances in the water
  And follows where it flows.
She climbs high over mountains,
  High, high, high,
And often when you look at her
  She seems to wink an eye.
    A star.

When nights are murky
Witches do most,
But when is a turkey
Most like a ghost?

When he is a-goblin'.

You surely haven't got it yet.
It's something you don't want to get.
But if you had it, you would not
Take the world for such a spot.

A bald head.

Why is a cat
    That springs without warning
Longer at night
    Than he is in the morning?

       Because he is let out at night and taken in in the
       morning.

*

    Of all things, weak or strong,
      In lightness one is first,
    But if you try to hold it long
      You feel that you will burst.

      Your breath.

*

When you're sitting down
    Drinking tea from a cup,
What will you lose
    When you stand up?

    Your lap.

When off this creature's head is cut
You have a creature that will butt.

F-ox.

*

What could you put in a box
  With water filled to the lid
And locked with a couple of locks
  To make it weigh less than it did?

Holes.

*

What part of a room,
    Neither outside nor in,
Is as high as a broom
    But pale and thin?

A window.

*

What have you
  That a pin has too?
And no doubt about it
  You're both worse without it.

A head.

50

A man was locked in a room
    With just a piano in it.
How did he open the door
    And get out in less than a minute?

He played the piano until he found the right key.

Legs like a kangaroo,
Ears like a mule,
Tail like a powder puff,
And runs like a fool.

A rabbit.

*

This you may answer
Perhaps in a hurry.
When is a blackberry
Not a blackberry?

When it is green.

*

Pink and violet,
Blue and lemony green,
It's not between the covers
Of your mother's magazine.
If you trap it in a room,
You may catch it near the door,
But it will be a catch
That's not been made before.

A rainbow.

How can you travel
   Fairly fast
Yet never get far
   From the first place you passed?

Go back and forth in a swing.

53

Tell me what nut,
   When nails are gone,
You might hang
   A picture on.

               The walnut.

*

You know the moon
   Is like a cheese,
But what nut
   Is like a sneeze?

      The cashew nut.

*

What nut is there
   That must have shrunk,
Since it ought to make
   A very good trunk?

         The chestnut.

*

Be so kind
   As to answer me.
What nut do you find
   On the shore of the sea?

        The beechnut.

Long legs,
  Croaking cries,
A bald head
  And bulging eyes.

A frog.

This one's known
    From Denver to Dover.
What's black and white
    And red all over?

    A blushing zebra.

*

Riddle me this and you'll tell
    What clouds are hiding.
Why are clouds like people
    Horseback riding?

    They both hold the rains (reins).

*

The more it dries
    Round people or pets,
To no one's surprise
    The wetter it gets.

    A towel.

You know about Humpty Dumpty,
But tell me this in a minute.
How can your pocket be empty
And still have something in it?

It can have a hole in it.

＊

When is a dog
That is yellow and brown
Most likely to enter
A house in town?

When the door is open.

＊

Roly Poly did something rash.
He rolled off a wall and hit with a splash.
And almost as soon as off he rolled
Roly Poly turned into gold.

An egg.

Boy with a toy,
  Girl with a curl,
What's the best way
  To catch a squirrel?

Climb a tree and act like a nut.

*

Are you able to guess
  What can fill a whole house
And still weigh less
  Than a tiny mouse?

Smoke.

*

What travels faster
  Than creatures with toes
But touches nothing
  As it goes?

Your voice.

*

Lollipop, lollipop,
  Buy it in the candy shop.
Why is it so like a horse
  Running around a big race course?

The more you lick it the faster it goes.

When this conundrum you have heard,
  Please don't hurry.
Now tell me what's the longest word
  In the dictionary.

Smiles—there's a mile between the first and
last letters.

Thrown at the sky, it drops,
  Which isn't so rare.
But thrown on the ground, it hops
  Back into the air.

A rubber ball.

*

What has a horn
That serves to warn
And is more dangerous
Than an octopus
Yet nicer by far
Than octopi are?

An automobile.

*

How can you keep from getting
  That sharp pain in the eye
Whenever you drink cocoa?
  At least it's something to try.

Take the spoon out of the cup.

If you know any history
    This won't be any mystery.
In fact, I think you're almost bound
    To know where kings are usually crowned.
On the head.

What do you have
    And sometimes lose
That houses have
    And carpenters use?
        Nails.

What is it that always
   Goes up in town
And gets left in hallways
   When the rain comes down?

An umbrella.

*

Why do Eskimos have air
That's always fresh beyond compare?

Because it is kept on ice.

*

How many fried eggs
Can the giant Long Legs
Eat like a lummox
When his huge stomach's
Empty completely
And still do it neatly?

Only one—then his stomach isn't empty, and the
second egg he always drops on his necktie.

The answer to this
    Could make you explode,
But why does a rooster
    Cross the road?
                    To get on the other side.

*

Comes in at every door,
    Comes in at every crack,
Runs round and round and round some more,
    But never leaves a track.
            The wind.

*

    Forty feet long
        With lots of hairs,
    It loves a good song
        And always eats pears.
                A forty-foot, hairy, song-loving pear-eater.

*

        I am so small
            And afraid of the night
        That always at dark
            I light up my light.
                    A firefly.

If you saw a bird in an apple tree
  Where not the slightest breeze stirred,
How could you shake down an apple for me
  Without disturbing the bird?
    By waiting till he flew away.

With which hand,
  Now you tell me,
Should you stir
  Your cup of tea?

With neither—most people use a spoon.

*

A long and legless fellow
  Who lives in a deep dark den,
He's more afraid of a rooster
  Than of a thousand men.

A worm.

*

What is so airy
  That hands can't take it,
Though one little word
  Is enough to break it?

Silence.

*

Why are good farmers,
  Every one born,
Kind to their cows
  But cruel to their corn?

They always pull its ears.

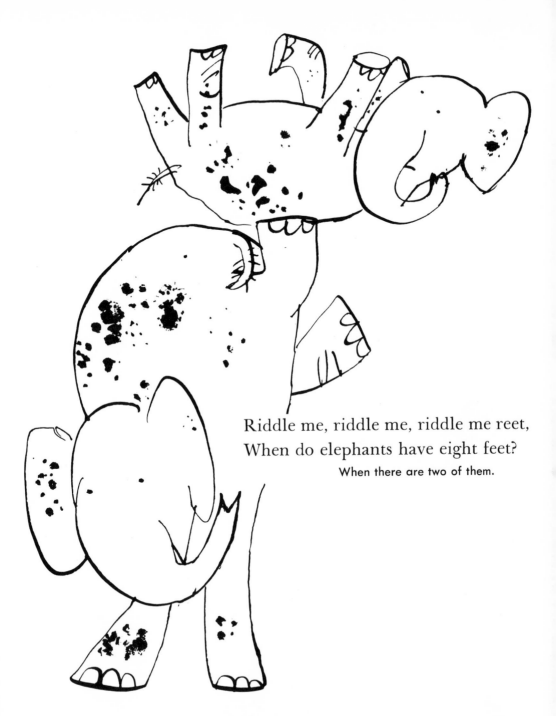

Riddle me, riddle me, riddle me reet,
When do elephants have eight feet?

When there are two of them.

Hush your silly giggling.
    Hush your silly talk.
Tell me what is musical
    About an icy walk.

If you don't C-sharp, you'll B-flat.

*

What crosses the land
    From coast to coast
But continues to stand
    As still as a post?

The highway.

*

What is it that surely
    Belongs to you
But that your friends use
    Much more than you do?

Your name.

*

Ragged rascal, reach for the stars!
Can you spell that without any r's?

T, H, A, T.

On a very empty stomach
  Is it safe to write a letter,
Or on a stomach that is full
  Can you write a letter better?
  It's usually better to write it on paper.

What's the difference,
   My, oh my,
Between a monkey
   And a sigh?

A sigh means "Oh, dear," and a monkey means you,
  dear!

Runs East and West
  And North and South,
Has many sharp teeth
  But hasn't a mouth.

A saw.

*

Crooked as a mountain railroad,
  Flatter than a dinner plate,
Forty thousand locomotives
  Couldn't ever pull it straight.

A river.

*

How many legs are there on a mule
  If you decide to make a rule
That lets you call the mule's tail a leg?
  Please answer me this, though I wink as I beg.

Only four—calling the mule's tail a leg doesn't make it a leg.

What is it that farmers
Highly prize
That has four legs
And also flies?

A horse in the summertime.

*

When a carpenter starts a new house
And considers every detail,
Tell me, if you're not a mouse,
Where he strikes the first nail.

On the head.

*

What's the difference
On July the Fourth
Between the South Pole
And the North?

All the difference in the world.

*

What has panes
But doesn't ache,
Is very hard
But easy to break?

A window.

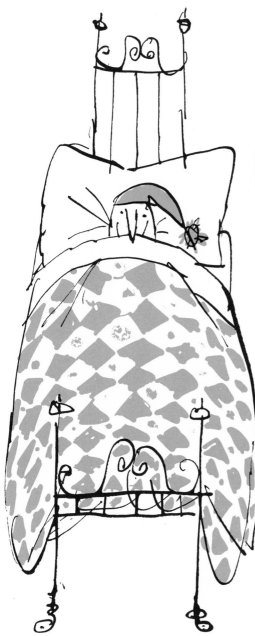

A man was locked up
    From spring to fall
In a room with a calendar,
    Bed, and that's all,
And none brought food
    To sell or give.
How in the world did
    The poor man live?

He drank from the spring in the bed
and ate dates off the calendar.

You could learn this
Just bobbing a cork.
How many big men
Have been born in New York?

None—only babies.

*

Riddle me, riddle me, riddle me ree,
How many hairs in a cat's tail? Whee!

None—they are all on the outside.

*

To keep his temper
A doctor must try
Especially hard.
Do you know why?

He can't afford to lose his patients.

*

The eight words below
Cannot be changed.
What sense do they show
The way they're arranged?

stand   take   to   world
   I   you   throw   the

I understand you undertake to overthrow the underworld.

How could you fall in the dirt
From a hundred-foot ladder
And luckily not get hurt
Or feel much sadder?

By falling off the first rung.

75

I'm sometimes strong and sometimes weak,
But I am nobody's fool.
For there is no language I can't speak
Though I never went to school.

An echo.

*

What is the difference,
If you will,
Between these two—
A hill and a pill?

A hill is hard to get up, but a pill is hard to get down.

*

What can you see
Down in the lake
That's always free
But that no one can take?

The moon.

*

Which do you think is bigger,
And please do not say "Maybe,"
Mrs. Bigger herself
Or Mrs. Bigger's baby?

Her baby is a little Bigger.

Three large ladies heard it thunder.
Three large ladies all got under
One small umbrella, or tried to get.
Why didn't the three large ladies get wet?

It didn't rain.

What two beaux,
    Not easy to love,
Can no young lady
    Rid herself of?

Her elbows.

*

Why does an Indian Big Chief wear
Many bright feathers in his hair?

To keep his wigwam.

*

England, Ireland, Scotland, Wales,
What has no head but oodles of tails?

A big book of stories.

*

First you picked a lemon,
    Then I picked a lime,
But what is it that always
    We do at the very same time?

Grow older.

*

I've a head and a tail
    But almost no middle.
I'm bright or I'm brown
    And I'm worth a little.
Head's up and tail's down,
    Now you have a riddle.

A penny.

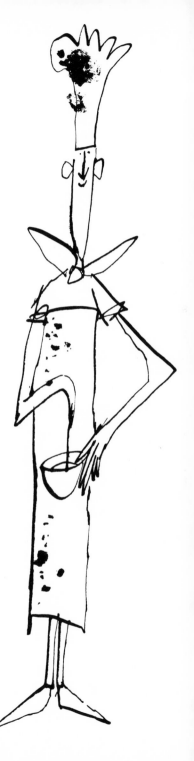

Though some are fat
    And some are lean,
Why are cooks
    'Most always mean?

Because they beat the eggs and whip the cream.

Three copycats sat by a pool
    Till one jumped in to get himself cool.
Now that I have given a clue,
    How many were left, according to you?

None, because they were all copycats.

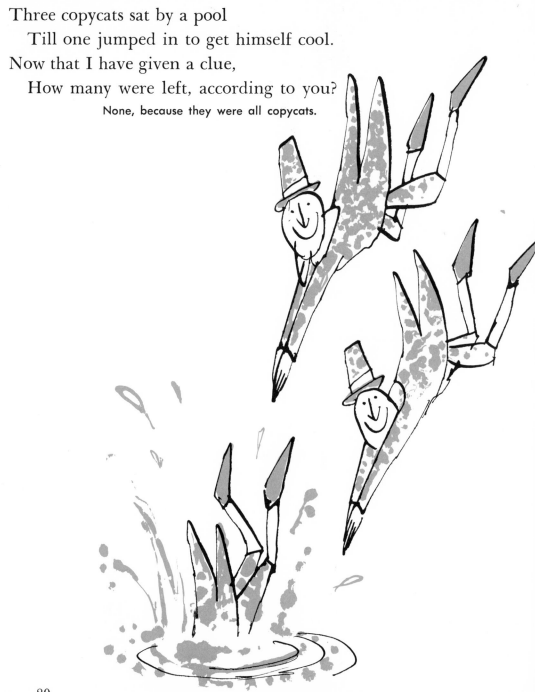

According to all hearsay
    What did Paul Revere say
When he, who seldom lied,
    Finished his famous ride?
        "Whoa!"

*

Exactly how much
    Dirt is there
In a hole a foot deep
    And two feet square?
        None.

*

Why are tennis players,
    The weaker and the stronger,
Not using tennis rackets
    Any longer?
        They are long enough already.

If this doesn't make you laugh,
    It'll get your goat.
What's worse than a grown giraffe
    With a sore throat?

        A grown centipede with sore feet.

*

Of those who see through this riddle,
    The answers are right without failure.
What is found in the middle
    Of America and Australia?

        The answer's R (see line two).

*

You probably know what you say
    When your shin is kicked,
But what does an envelope say
    When it is licked?

        It just shuts up and says nothing.

*

If cats have many kittens
    And just as many lives,
What do we have that's always coming
    But never really arrives?

        Tomorrow—when it arrives, it is today.

Eight crows in a tree,
   All guilty of theft.
If a man shoots three,
   How many are left?

None—the others would fly away.

What letter has never yet
Been found in the alphabet?
The one you put in the mail box.

*

Rat a tat tat, rat a tat tat,
What makes an elephant's feet so flat?
Jumping out of trees.

*

Emeralds and diamonds
Lost by the moon
Are found by the sun
And picked up soon.
Dewdrops.

*

One man speared a big oak tree,
Then rode his horse right through it.
Another rode up and jumped the same tree,
Just to show that he could do it.
The third one uprooted the same oak tree
As if there were nothing to it.
Which was the strongest one of the three
As seen by their deeds at the big oak tree?
How could there be an answer to such a big lie?

Chook-chook-chook, chook-chook-chook,
Cock-a-doodle-doo!
Chook-chook-chook, chook-chook-chook,
Do you know these two?

A rooster and a hen.

85

In spite of all
    His mother said,
Why did Paul
    Take a hammer to bed?
            So he could hit the hay.

This one came right out of the zoo,
    And it's a thriller.
Would you rather have a lion chase you
    Or a gorilla?
            I'd rather have him chase the gorilla.

＊

If three ripe tomatoes
    Are up on a shelf,
Which one is a cowboy
    Like yourself?
            None of them—they're all redskins.

Speak up at once,
   If you have a hunch,
And tell me who has
   The most people for lunch.
       A cannibal.

*

That you know this, I'd be willing to bet.
Why was the little strawberry upset?
       Because his mother and daddy got into a jam.

*

Hippo-hippo-potamuses,
They're almost as big as buses.
What do they have, and this is true,
That none of the other animals do?
       Little hippopotamuses.

Two splendid horses,
    One black and one white,
Run after each other
    Day and night.
        Day and night.

*

Why are promises
    Like little boys
Who at the movies
    Make lots of noise?
        The sooner they are carried out, the better.

*

What word is it
    That all along
Children have been
    Pronouncing wrong?
        Wrong.

*

All are cold and very skinny
    And all are of a similar size,
But those with eyes don't have any heads
    And those with heads don't have any eyes.
    Needles and pins.

I know that you've heard alarms
  Of many queer things,
But what has eight legs, two arms,
  Three heads, and wings?

A man on horseback with a canary on his head.

North, South,
   Opens like a mouth.
Snip, snap,
   Closes like a trap.

A pair of scissors.

*

It isn't my sister
  Nor my brother,
But still it's the child
  Of my father and mother.

Myself.

*

They make no sound
And cause no pain,
Yet strike each other
Again and again.

The eyelids.

You've had one, I'll bet,
    Yes-sir-ee.
It walks on one foot
    And hums like a bee.

A top.

We're like two flowers,
   But when we bloom
We fill half the world,
   Including your room.

The sun and the moon.

92

Tell me, now,
Can you say
Why you should avoid
The letter A?

It makes m-e-n m-e-a-n.

*

When it comes to questions
I have rather many,
Like why is a dog
A lot like a penny?

Each has a head and a tail.

*

Do you know what
Is the very first thing
You're going to plant
In your garden this spring?

Your foot.

*

You've heard some wild ones,
But oh brother!
What did one flea
Say to the other?

"Shall we walk or take a dog?"

If you answer this
   I'll be fit to be tied.
Which side of a pie
   Is the left side?

The side that isn't eaten.

The little girl opened the icebox
   Because she thought it a nice box.
But when she saw it was empty that day
   What seven letters did the little girl say?
            O,I,C,U,R,M,T.

*

What makes more noise,
   Early or late,
Than a squealing pig
   Caught under a gate?
       Two squealing pigs.

*

I'll bet that you,
   Alack alas,
With just three letters
   Can't spell dried grass.
       H,A,Y.

*

Old King Cole had a daughter
   Who could outspell her betters.
Let's see if you can spell hard water
   And only use three letters.
      I,C,E.

What floats in the water
As light as can be,
Yet thousands of men
Cannot lift it free?
A bubble.

*

Why is a pony
Halfway through a gate
A lot like a penny?
I can wait.
Because his head is on one side, his tail on the other.

*

Why did the little boy
Who acted like a monkey
Seem to get such joy
From standing behind the donkey?
He thought he'd get a kick out of it.

*

When Columbus discovered America,
When he first sighted land,
What did the great explorer see
Upon his right hand?
Five fingers.

It looks like your twin
And you see it a lot,
But you can speak
And it cannot.

Your reflection in a mirror.

With riddling words
We like a good hinter,
But why do birds like
To fly south for the winter?

Because it's too far to walk.

*

In the word *cloves*
Can you guess
Why, though apart,
C thinks of S?

Because there is love between them.

*

If it isn't your desire,
Don't answer this at all.
But can anyone jump higher
Than a thirty-foot wall?

Of course—a wall can't jump.

*

Since you are one who knows about plants
And likes to watch them grow,
What would come up, in addition to ants,
If you planted an angry crow?

Crow-cusses.

Where could you put a candle,
　　When in a room with your friends,
So that all but you could see it?
　　And don't say "That depends."
On your head.

What word of only three syllables,
And those as soft as down,
Has in it six and twenty letters
Scattered all over town?

Alphabet.

✳

What wears clothes in the summertime
When it's too hot to scold,
But none at all in the wintertime
When winds are blowing cold?

A tree.

✳

I ask you nicely
Without demanding—
What is taller
Sitting than standing?

A dog.

✳

Thousands of shining knights
Go with their radiant Queen,
Yet when the golden Prince appears
They flee till none are seen.

The moon and the stars that disappear when the sun comes up.

Bill bet Bob that he could eat
  More oysters than he in an hour.
Bill ate ninety-nine, but still Bob beat.
  How many did Bob devour?

He ate a hundred and won.

While Johnny Darling took a swim,
  Someone took his clothes.
What then did Johnny come home in,
  Dewy as a rose?

Twilight.

*

  Why does the ocean
    Need a lotion,
  And why does it roar
    From shore to shore?

It always has crabs in its bed.

*

Horses have colts
  And cows calve,
But what kind of ears
  Do engines have?

Engineers.

*

  Bill's mother knit him three socks
    While he was at camp one year.
  Why did she do such a thing,
    Which even she thought rather queer?

Because Bill wrote he had grown another foot.

Some know whom Australia
Was founded by,
But who knows what Australia
Is bounded by?

Kangaroos.

A man out boating
Saw an egg floating
  Down the river's middle.
Tell me where from
The egg would have come
  And you will have answered a riddle.

From a hen.

*

If you have exactly a hundred male deer
  All in a lot
Along with a hundred female pigs,
  What have you got?

A hundred sows and bucks.

*

You know this,
  So don't be forlorn.
What does a worm
  Do in the corn?

Goes in one ear and out the other.

*

A baby rabbit's nose is tiny,
But tell me why it's also shiny.

Because the powder puff is at the wrong end.

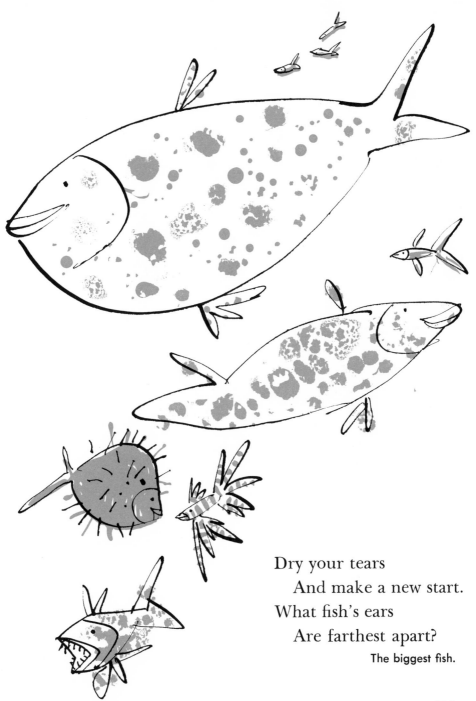

Dry your tears
And make a new start.
What fish's ears
Are farthest apart?

The biggest fish.

Not even the wisest king
   Could answer this one soon.
How many balls of string
   Would it take to reach the moon?
     Only one, if it were long enough.

Bought by the yard,
   Worn by the foot,
All over the room
   This thing can be put.

A carpet.

*

Looking hard
   With you and me,
Exactly what
   Did Tennessee?

Just what Arkansaw.

What strongbox do you bear
That you often fill with air?

Your chest.

*

What great difference can you see
Between a buffalo and a flea?

A buffalo can have fleas, but a flea can't have buffaloes.

Tell me, tell me,
  Have you heard
The three best ways
  Of spreading the word?

Telephone, telegraph, and tell a secret.

*

When you were a baby
  You went by-by,
But when, O when
  Did the little fly fly?

When the spider spied 'er.

*

What kind of umbrella
  Does Mrs. Delaney
Carry along
  When it is rainy?

A wet one.

*

The happiest vowel,
  The one full of bliss,
Is—you tell me.
  You're bound to guess this.

I, because it's in the middle of bliss.

When can you expect
  To be quite correct
Although you should wish
  To serve milk in a dish?

When you feed the cat.

My teeth are straight and shining white,
  So goes this rhythmic riddle,
And when folks hit them hard or light,
  I cry more than a little.

A piano.

*

What runs around
  A tree without stopping?
It's tireless and tough
  But can't stand chopping.

The bark.

*

On the farm
  Or in the town
What walks above us
  Upside down?

A fly on the ceiling.

*

What did the piano player say
  When someone said to him,
"Do you know your monkey is in my soup
  Trying to take a swim?"

He said, "No, but if you'll hum it I'll try to play it."

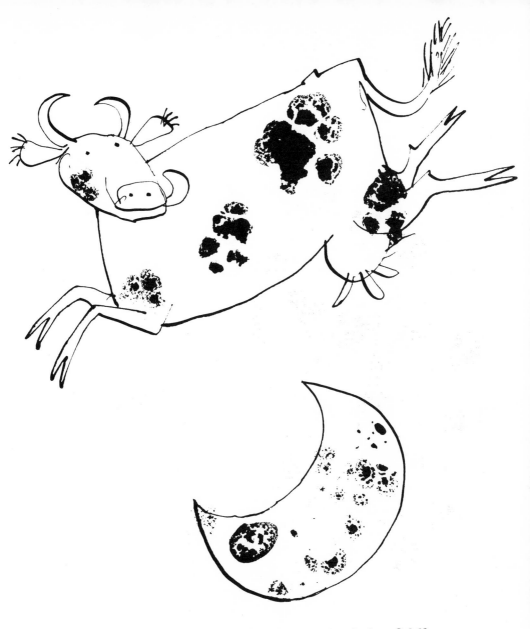

Hey diddle diddle, the cat and the fiddle,
Of course you know what that's in.
But do you know, says this little riddle,
When beef was the highest it's been?

When the cow jumped over the moon.

Why do you think
The figure 9
Is like a peacock
Proud and fine?

Without a tail, it is nothing.

Why is the letter U
Never serious,
Though U can be, it's true,
A bit mysterious?

It's always in the midst of fun.

*

Why is an island
Out in the sea
A whole lot like
The letter T?

Because it's in the middle of water.

What happened when a lady
On a boat,
In the refrigerator
Found a goat?

The goat turned to butt 'er.

*

Guess again—you've done your worst.
Why is a candle flame like thirst?

A little water will end them both.

What has two hookers
And two big lookers,
Four hangers-down,
Four runners-around,
And when it's hotter
A long fly-swatter?

A cow.

*

Out in the woods
I saw Little Mac
Walking along
With a house on his back.

A turtle.

*

What number is larger,
And please don't frown,
When you turn it
Upside down?

6 becomes 9.

*

What's smaller than any mouse
That lives in a wee hole
And often comes into the house
By means of the keyhole?

The key.

114

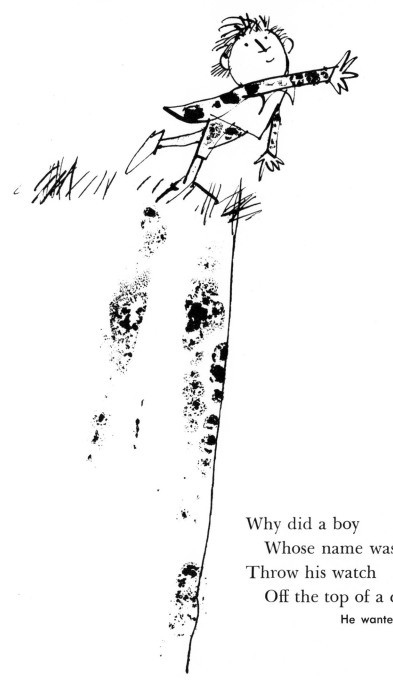

Why did a boy
   Whose name was Biff
Throw his watch
   Off the top of a cliff?

      He wanted to see time fly.

What runs around
    The whole big yard,
Yet never moves?
    This riddle's not hard.

The fence.

* *

What overtakes you
    Though you flee it
And lays you low
    Though you never see it?

Sleep.

*

You don't have to break a water keg
    In order to drink and drink well,
But how can you possibly eat an egg
    Unless you break the eggshell?

Have someone else break it.

* *

Please take your seats
    And say without fail
What animal eats
    And drinks with its tail.

All do—no animal removes its tail before eating and drinking.

116

What do the children
In China call
Young yellow cats
When they are small?

Kittens.

Why is it that you find a ball
That you are looking for
Always in the last place of all
That you decide to explore?

> Because when you find it you stop looking for it.

*

Will anything else
Make you squirm
Like biting an apple
And finding a worm?

> Finding half a worm.

*

Fire won't burn me.
Water won't drown me.
Wherever I am
It's cold all around me.

> Ice.

* *

Why might it be good,
Though it mightn't, of course,
If a black widow spider
Were big as a horse?

> Well, if one should bite you, you could ride it to the hospital.

Three men fell overboard
  And none of them stayed dry,
But only two got their hair wet.
  Can you tell me why?

The other man was bald.

Why is a warm winter day,
  When you can ride your bicycle,
Not at all a good day
  For the character of an icicle?

Because it turns it into an eavesdropper.

* *

I'm like you
  And you're like me,
But when is a brook
  Like the letter T?

When you have to cross it.

* *

Since your manners are mild,
  How would you ever be able
To stop a naughty child
  From throwing food at the table?

Feed him on the floor.

* *

What odd number,
  Please try to guess,
Is bound to be even
  Without the S?

S-even.

Here's an easy
  Riddle to guess.
What question can never
  Be answered "Yes"?

"Are you asleep?"

When the little boy said, "Mother deer,
   May eye go out to play?
The son is bright, the heir is clear,"
   What did his mother say?
       "Neigh."

*

Dark underneath,
   White outside,
The last hot spell
   He almost died.
       A wolf in sheep's clothing.

*

Afterwards
   We still will sing,
But what is the end
   Of everything?
       The letter G.

*

Cats are annoyed by noise
   And they don't like much moisture,
But what is the one kind of noise
   That even annoys an oyster?
       A noisy noise annoys an oyster.

On land and sea and in the air,
Riddles, riddles everywhere.
Here in this book you've found a few.
And now,

What's read
All the way through?

This book and you.

NOTE

In one of the most famous of ancient Greek myths, the Sphinx asks Oedipus a riddle: "What goes on four legs in the morning, and two at noon, and on three when evening comes?" "Man," the hero answers, "who crawls, then walks, then uses a cane," and so he begins his disastrous career as King of Thebes. For many centuries, both before and after Oedipus, people all over the world have been asking and guessing riddles with far less unhappy results. They have also been making verses that ask riddles, with results that are sometimes quite delightful. Most of the verse riddles included in this book, I have made from prose originals that have for generations been part of American and British folklore.

The most comprehensive collection of folk riddles in our language is Archer Taylor's monumental *English Riddles from Oral Tradition* (University of California Press, 1951), which includes an extensive bibliography of riddle collections. Two excellent less formal collections of folk riddles, mostly prose, are Carl Withers and Sula Benet's *The American Riddle Book* (Abelard-Schuman, 1954) and Bennett Cerf's *Riddle-De-Dee* (Random House, 1962).